Simply Salad

RECIPES FROM THE SOUTH-WEST

HEATHER CORBETT

TOR MARK REDRUTH

Published by Tor Mark,
United Downs Industrial Estate, St Day,
Redruth, Cornwall TR16 5HY

www.tormark.co.uk

ISBN 978 085025 411 2

cover image © Cadmium

Printed in Great Britain by R Booth Ltd,
The Praze, Penryn, Cornwall TR10 8AA

Other books about local food & drink

Clotted Cream, Carolyn Martin (Tor Mark)
Cornish Cheeses, Caryl Minson (Tor Mark)
Cornish Recipes, Ann Pascoe (Tor Mark)
Devonshire Cookbook, Margaret Wilson (Bossiney Books)
Farmhouse Cider, Bob Bunker (Bossiney Books)
Fast and Fresh Recipes from the South-West, Heather Corbett (Tor Mark)
Fish Recipes from the South-West, Heather Corbett (Tor Mark)
The Herb Book, Deborah Fowler and Sally Cuckson (Truran)
New Cornish Cookbook, Margaret Wilson (Tor Mark)
The Pasty Book, Hettie Merrick (Tor Mark)
Smuggling Recipes, Carolyn Martin (Bossiney Books)
Sprouting, Deborah Fowler (Truran)
Traditional Somerset Recipes, Carolyn Martin (Bossiney Books)
Vegetarian Recipes from the West Country, Margaret Wilson (Bossiney Books)

Contents

Introduction

Salads above all need to be simple. They celebrate a happy blend of ingredients, where all the components are defined, making a good contrast with one another in four ways: taste, colour, shape and texture. It is good if there is an element of surprise as well – an unexpected use of one of these contrasts. Salads always have a dressing – this is sometimes used to harmonise the ingredients and sometimes to make a piquant contrast.

Salads can be large or small – large if they are the main course, small if they are a starter, a lunch or a side dish to offset a completely different main course. They can be cooked – or not, or more often a mixture of cooked and raw ingredients; they can be vegetarian, or not; they can include some kind of carbohydrate padding, such as rice, pasta or potatoes – or not; they can include fruit – or not; they can be composed of completely fresh ingredients – or not – store cupboard items such as a few walnuts or cornichons, or a few leftovers can make a wonderful contrast. Herbs are a wonderful added ingredient – adding a touch of freshness or surprise.

The important thing about salad is that above all it is creative – you can have fun putting it together, imagining what ingredients will work successfully together and what will not. Salmagundy or salat have been with us since Elizabethan times. Now we are very health conscious and want to eat more raw foods and more vegetables so salad is the obvious answer. It celebrates what is available from season to season and what the local shops, the farmers' market or your own back garden can produce. Try to keep it simple so that the individual tastes come through clearly. These recipes all work as combinations of ingredients, but they are not intended to be prescriptive, simply

1

to give you ideas – try to mix and match as much as you can using what is available, what is good and what you like.

Over the last few years the variety of available lettuce and salad leaves has increased and sprouting seeds and beans have been added to the repertoire. There is now a range of named tomatoes, each variety fit for a different use because of its size, flavour or texture. On the whole I have not named varieties, leaving it to you to choose what seems best when you go shopping or picking. We are no longer afraid to eat vegetables raw and herbs are readily available in supermarkets if we do not have them in our gardens – the range and choice for salad ingredients is enormous.

I have given the recipes for four basic and contrasting dressings, suitable for different salad ingredients; great fun can be had in playing with new oils or vinegars. Experiment with dressing ingredients – different oils, different vinegars or juices, mustards or other ingredients – sugars, honey, herbs.

Try to celebrate and enjoy what is in season; vegetables which have been flown half way across the world cannot have many nutrients or flavour left by the time you open the vacuum pack.

Salads are very rewarding to prepare – they are quick, fun, tasty and pretty and often surprise your family or guests – what more could you want!

Lettuce, Tomato, Cucumber

When I was a girl, this is what salad was, served in a bowl, the lettuce cut into 4 or 6 so that everyone had some heart, the tomatoes cut into quarters and the cucumber into chunks. It was served with salad cream and usually accompanied by cold meat, either ham or something left from the Sunday joint. These days we have a very different take on it, but nevertheless it is a good base, either as a starter or to accompany a main course.

For 4
1 lettuce – any sort will do of the plainer variety – cabbage, Webb's, Romaine, Little Gem
6 medium tomatoes, sliced
5cm cucumber, sliced
4 tablespoons dressing
2 tablespoons mixed, finely chopped herbs

Break up the lettuce into leaves – if the leaves are large break them into 2 or 3. With a sharp knife, slice the tomatoes into thin slices. Slice the cucumber in the same way. Now comes the crucial difference from the past, add a few herbs – basil or mint would be good roughly chopped up and then add a dressing. Choose one you fancy from pp7–10. Now comes the most important thing – gently mix the salad by using your salad servers to lift up the leaves and mix the other ingredients around. Everything should have a light coating of the lovely dressing.

Basic Salads

Summer Salad

This salad takes advantage of the abundance of salad ingredients available very fresh during the summer. Use an unusual variety of lettuce or mixed leaves, such as baby spinach, rocket, lamb's lettuce or mizuna. If you cannot get French beans substitute broad beans or sugar snap peas. Radishes grow very easily, so it is worth planting a few radish seeds even if you do not have a vegetable garden, so that you can pick a handful at will. The addition of fresh herbs makes this a very fresh salad. Choose mint, French parsley and a very small quantity of coriander.

For 4
a colanderful of mixed leaves or a lettuce
200gm French beans, podded broad beans or sugar snap peas
12 radishes, whole if small or roughly sliced if larger
6 spring onions, roughly chopped
2 dessertspoons mixed herbs, finely chopped
4 tablespoons dressing

Carefully wash and spin the mixed leaves – I find salad spinners very good at getting rid of the water – much better than other methods. Prepare the French beans or their alternatives and plunge them into a saucepan of boiling water for 3 minutes, no longer, they need to retain some of their crunchiness. Put them into a bowl and spoon over some of the dressing, so that it soaks into the vegetable as it cools. Prepare the radishes and the spring onions as above and add to the leaves, with the herbs. Then add the vegetables and the rest of the dressing. Choose any dressing from pp7–10; I would choose the simplicity of the French dressing.

Winter Salad

This salad uses vegetables which are freely and easily available during the winter. Traditionally hard white cabbage is used for that all-time favourite coleslaw, and although this salad is based on that I prefer to use savoy cabbage, if I can, both for its colour and its texture.

For 4
½ cabbage, either white or savoy
3 middle-sized sticks celery, chopped
2 medium carrots, grated
2 medium potatoes, cubed
2 medium red onions, finely chopped
4 tablespoons dressing

Start with the potatoes. Dice these into 2cm cubes and then boil until just cooked, drain, place in your salad bowl and pour the dressing over them to allow it to soak in a little as the potatoes cool. You may use any of the dressings on pp7–10; I prefer the yogurt and mayonnaise dressing or the sour cream dressing for this recipe. Next cut out the hard core of the cabbage and slice thinly, chop up the celery into small pieces, grate the carrot and finely chop the onion – I suggest red onion for its colour and because it is less strong. Mix all the ingredients carefully together. You may like to add a dessertspoon of sultanas or walnuts to add little surprises of flavour and texture.

Basic Salads

Store Cupboard Salad

This is a basic store cupboard salad using ingredients that I assume most people will have readily available. More about store cupboard salads on pp35 and 36. The base for this salad is always some sort of lettuce, mixed leaves or sprouting beans or seeds, or cabbage, savoy or white. This is a very useful salad when you are in a hurry and yet want to make your meal seem a little more exciting.

For 4
Lettuce or similar
1 tablespoon pine nuts
1 tablespoon sun blush tomatoes from a jar
16 olives from a jar
8 cornichons or 4 gerkins from a jar
12 cubes of Feta cheese from a jar
4 tablespoons basic French dressing

Tear up the lettuce or chop the cabbage as appropriate. Mix in the other ingredients and add your dressing. Basic French dressing is probably the best for this group of ingredients.

Basic French Dressing

The dressing that is put on a salad will either make or break it. You cannot go far wrong by using the basic recipe for French dressing, sometimes called vinaigrette.

To dress one salad for 4
6 dessertspoons extra virgin olive oil
2 dessertspoons wine vinegar
½ teaspoon sugar
½ teaspoon mustard powder
1 clove garlic, crushed (can be optional)
salt and black pepper to taste

Start with the sugar, garlic and mustard, then add the olive oil and stir hard, then add the wine vinegar and the salt and pepper and stir hard again. If you do not use immediately, you will need to stir again before adding to the salad.

Notes:
Do use extra virgin olive oil: it does make a difference, both in flavour and thickness, so that it stays on the leaves and does not drain to the bottom of the bowl – what a waste!

There is a wide variety of vinegars; in this recipe use either white or red wine vinegar – make your choice according to the strength of the flavour of your salad ingredients – white wine vinegar for the more delicate flavours and red for those which are stronger. Lemon juice instead of vinegar makes a good change. This recipe uses mustard powder, because it thickens the dressing a little; French mustard and French grain mustard are both good when you want to add texture as well as flavour.

Dressings

Yogurt and Mayonnaise Dressing

This is a richer dressing than the basic vinaigrette. I make no apologies for using commercial mayonnaise, as long as it is good quality. Making mayonnaise is time-consuming and can be fraught with difficulty as it is inclined to 'split' – there is the added problem that it uses raw eggs which can be a problem for some people. It is worth making for special occasions, such as when you serve a whole cold salmon for a party. This dressing is not as rich as plain mayonnaise, the yogurt giving a lightness, a slight sharpness and reducing the calories a little. Having said that there is nothing like a lovely potato salad made with new potatoes and mayonnaise!

To dress one salad for 4
2 tablespoons mayonnaise
2 tablespoons natural yogurt
1 tablespoon lemon juice or white wine vinegar
½ teaspoon sugar
½ teaspoon mustard powder
1 tablespoon finely chopped mixed herbs – parsley, dill, mint
salt and black pepper to taste

Mix together the sugar and the mustard powder, slowly stir in the yogurt. Add the mayonnaise, which will take a little vigorous stirring to get rid of any lumps, then add the lemon juice or wine vinegar and season to taste. Be careful not to overdo this as the mayonnaise will have already been seasoned. Add the herbs – more parsley than either dill or mint.

Sweet and Sour Tomato Dressing

This dressing adds an element of surprise to what can appear to be a very ordinary salad. Once you have used it a few times you will see what ingredients it enhances – such things as avocado, leek, cucumber, white cabbage, courgettes, carrot – the list is long, once you start experimenting.

To dress one salad for 4
4 tablespoons extra virgin olive oil
1½ tablespoons red wine vinegar
1 dessertspoon tomato purée
1 tablespoon sultanas
1 clove of garlic crushed (can be optional)
1 teaspoon grain mustard
salt and black pepper to taste

Mix together the tomato purée, mustard and the garlic. Then add the olive oil and the red wine vinegar. You will need to stir this vigorously to disperse the tomato purée. Finally add the sultanas and the salt and pepper to taste. It is good to leave this to stand for a few minutes so that the sultanas plump up with the dressing. If you do let the dressing stand you will have to stir it again to fully mix the ingredients.

Dressings

Herby Sour Cream Dressing

This dressing is much fresher and sharper than the yogurt and mayonnaise dressing listed on p8. It goes well with potatoes, cucumber, mushrooms, tomatoes, asparagus, peas and beans. Choose herbs that will offset the ingredients of the salad; chives are always good as is parsley, either French or curled; dill gives a Scandanavian flavour, while oregano or basil are more Mediterranean.

To dress one salad for 4
4 tablespoons soured cream
1½ tablespoons lemon juice or white wine vinegar
1 teaspoon French mustard
½ teaspoon sugar
1 clove of garlic crushed
1 tablespoon mixed herbs
salt and black pepper to taste

First mix together the garlic, sugar, and mustard. Then add the lemon juice or white wine vinegar, stirring carefully. Next add the soured cream and the herbs and finally the salt and black pepper.

This dressing will not keep in the same way as the previous three dressings, because of the fresh soured cream – one day in the fridge at most.

The Idea of Take 5 Salads

'Take 5' salads are for starters, light lunches or as side salads to complement a main course. The idea is to take five ingredients only and add a dressing.

The reason for five ingredients is on the one hand to limit the number of ingredients – so often in restaurants a salad is produced which looks wonderful because it has many ingredients and looks exciting, but where in fact the ingredients are fighting one another or are not complementary and so all you taste is a muddle. The other reason for taking five ingredients is exactly the opposite – it is all too easy to make a 'simple' salad of lettuce, tomato and cucumber, yet with the addition of an extra couple of ingredients the salad is lifted from the mundane to the sublime.

In Take 5 salads lettuce or mixed leaves are not usually the dominant ingredient – they may be included, but only as a balanced partner to the other ingredients. What really matters is trying to get a contrast of colour, texture and taste.

These salads should be dressed lightly with the dressing being trailed across them. Occasionally a sprinkling of one particular herb will highlight the flavour.

The next four pages give examples of the fun of inventing a Take 5 salad. They are all served on individual plates.

Take 5

Green Take 5

For 4
1 green apple
⅓ cucumber
1 green pepper
2 Little Gem lettuces, each cut in half
16 seedless grapes
3 tablespoons basic French dressing

Cut the cucumber, the apple and the green pepper into small chunks and place next to the ½ Little Gem lettuce on each of the plates. Cut the grapes in half and sprinkle over the other salad ingredients. Dress delicately.

Red Take 5

For 4
4 medium tomatoes
1 red pepper
16 radishes
8 small beetroot from a jar
2 tablespoons walnut pieces
3 tablespoons sweet and sour tomato dressing

Cut the tomatoes into chunks, roughly cut the red pepper and cut the radishes into 3 or 4 pieces. Mix together; add 2 tablespoons of the dressing. When you are ready to serve, mix in the walnuts and the roughly chopped beetroot and spoon onto the plates. A tablespoon of chopped parsley sprinkled over the top would offset the colour well.

Egg and Mushrooms Take 5

For 4
4 hardboiled eggs
4cm cucumber, thinly sliced
200gm mushrooms, thinly sliced
16 sunblush tomatoes from a jar
2 handfuls rocket leaves
4 tablespoons basic French dressing

Place the rocket leaves on the plates as a base and then sprinkle with the sunblush tomatoes, the cucumber and the mushrooms, both thinly sliced and then trail the salad dressing over all – the mushrooms will soak up quite a lot of the dressing, especially if left for a few minutes. Place an egg, sliced as thinly as you can on top of each salad.

Grated Take 5

For 4
3 medium carrots, grated
a chunk of celeriac, grated
6cm cucumber, grated
8 anchovies from a tin
2 tablespoons walnut pieces
3 tablespoons yogurt and mayonnaise dressing

Place the grated vegetables close together on the plates in 3 little piles. Cut the anchovies up and sprinkle over the salad, then add the walnuts. Pour over the dressing sparingly, you do not want to drown the salad. A little chopped dill would be a good addition.

Take 5

Niçoise Take 5

For 4
2 handfuls mixed leaves or 1 lettuce
4 medium tomatoes, thinly sliced
16 black olives
140gm tinned tuna, lightly flaked
4 spring onions, chopped
4 tablespoons basic French dressing

Distribute the leaves or lettuce evenly amongst the plates, then add the tomatoes, olives and flaked tuna. Decorate with the spring onions. Spoon the dressing over all – it will take more than the other recipes. Decorate with some basil leaves.

Gorgonzola Take 5

For 4
2 sticks celery, roughly chopped
1 green pepper, roughly chopped
2 avocados, roughly chopped
150gm Gorgonzola or similar blue cheese, cubed
16 seedless grapes, cut in half
3 tablespoons herby sour cream dressing

Gently mix together all the ingredients and distribute amongst the plates. Pour a little of the sour cream dressing over each portion.

Salami Take 5

For 4
16 slices salami
12 chunks of artichoke from a jar
20 cherry tomatoes, halved
16 black olives
4 spring onions, chopped
3 tablespoons basic French dressing

Slice the salami into quarters and distribute amongst the plates and then decorate with the other ingredients. Dress delicately with the dressing. A little chopped mint would be an interesting addition.

Italian Take 5

For 4
2 handfuls of rocket leaves
4 tomatoes, thinly sliced
2 avocados, peeled an sliced
2 mozzarella cheeses, sliced
16 black olives
3 tablespoons French dressing made with balsamic rather than wine vinegar

Place the rocket on the plates as a base and then lay the tomatoes, mozzarella and avocados on top of it making an attractive pattern. Add the black olives and drizzle the dressing over all. Decorate with a few torn basil leaves.

Meal in a Bowl Salads

A Meal in a Bowl Salad

These salads are substantial main courses. They have lettuce or cabbage as a base with the addition of meat or fish and a variety of complementary vegetables, either raw or cooked. Bowl salads are served in one large bowl allowing people to eat as much as they choose. Beware these salad bowls can be moreish!

Smoked Chicken and Avocado Bowl Salad

This is a very soothing salad – all the ingredients are quite soft, although to varying degrees, so that the raw cabbage and the just cooked French beans add a little crunch. The sultanas add the surprise of sweetness.

For 4
3 breasts of smoked chicken
2 avocados
½ savoy cabbage, chopped, or a lettuce, torn
200gm French beans lightly boiled, chopped into 2cm pieces
2 spring onions, chopped
2 tablespoons sultanas
4 tablespoons yogurt and mayonnaise dressing

Cut each chicken breast into 4 or 5 and the avocados into chunks. The cabbage should be quite finely chopped. Mix all the ingredients together in one bowl and then add only so much dressing as needed to give a thin coating.

Smoked Mackerel Bowl Salad

Smoked mackerel are often forgotten about, yet they are readily available from fishmongers or supermarket fish counters and they keep well in the fridge for a few days, especially if they are vacuum packed. Try, if at all possible, to buy them from a local smoker as the flavour will be much better.

For 4
4 smoked mackerel fillets
3 sticks celery, chopped
1 apple, chopped
¼ white cabbage, chopped
4cm cucumber, roughly chopped
½ onion, finely chopped
4 tablespoons herby sour cream dressing

First chop the white cabbage quite finely and place in your salad bowl, then add the celery, finely chopped onion, the apple and the cucumber. Carefully flake the smoked mackerel and place on top. Gently pour or spoon over the dressing so that it touches all the ingredients, but does not immerse them.

Meal in a Bowl Salads

Hot Smoked Salmon Bowl Salad

Hot smoked salmon is a delight; it has a wonderful smoky flavour, yet the flesh has the density, texture and good flavour of fresh salmon. Please note it is not hot in temperature it has been 'hot' smoked – that is smoked and gently cooked at the same time, rather than 'cold' smoked where there is no heat source. If possible buy from a local smoker as the quality of the fish and the smoking will be better. This is a salad that sings in the spring because of the asparagus and the new potatoes.

For 4
4 medium sized pieces of hot smoked salmon
4cm cucumber, chopped
8 spears asparagus, lightly cooked
8 new potatoes, cooked and halved
4 spring onions, chopped
1 lettuce
4 tablespoons yogurt and mayonnaise dressing
1 lemon, quartered

Lay a base of lettuce leaves in the salad bowl; the larger leaves will need to be torn in half. Then add the cucumber, the new potatoes and the spring onions; carefully add enough of the dressing so that it coats the leaves. Then add the hot smoked salmon, broken into quite large pieces and decorate with the asparagus spears. Drizzle a little more dressing across the salmon and place the lemon quarters on top in case people need the juice to offset the richness of the salmon.

Waldorf in a Bowl Salad

This salad is a variation on Waldorf Salad which was originally created at the Waldorf Hotel in New York. I have always liked it because of the apple and the walnuts with mayonnaise which I find very unusual, but which complement a number of other ingredients, especially chicken or fish. Here I have used it with dried ham – a contrast in texture, colour and taste.

For 4
2 apples, chopped
2 tablespoons walnut pieces
¼ white cabbage, chopped
3 sticks celery, chopped
1 tablespoon sultanas
8 slices Bavarian, Parma or Serrano ham
4 tablespoons herby sour cream dressing

Carefully mix the first 5 ingredients together in the salad bowl and add the dressing. Then tear the dried ham slices into 2 or 3 pieces and push down into the salad, so they are discovered as little surprises as the salad is served and then eaten.

Meal in a Bowl Salads

Ham Salad with a Difference

This salad is reminiscent of that great English dish – boiled ham with broad beans and parsley sauce. It is important to use chunks of ham not slices of ham; the flavour of the ham will not come through with sliced ham.

For 4
250gm ham from a joint, cut into 1cm chunks
4 eggs, hardboiled, cut roughly
1 Cos lettuce or similar
4 tablespoons fresh broad beans, but frozen will substitute
2 spring onions, chopped
2 tablespoons chopped parsley
4 tablespoons yogurt and mayonnaise dressing

Break up the Cos lettuce so that the larger leaves are in 3 or 4 pieces. Boil the broad beans for 3 minutes – frozen beans are not as good, but are a reasonable substitute, as long as they are not allowed to get soft. Add the ham, beans, spring onions, eggs and parsley to the lettuce and mix together gently; add the dressing – just enough to cover lightly.

Vegetables Solo

This bowl salad celebrates vegetables fresh from the garden or market. In some ways it is like the ubiquitous Russian salad, but so much nicer! Although there are herbs in the dressing, it needs the additional herbs as well to highlight the green freshness that the dish relies upon.

For 4
8 new potatoes, cooked and cut into cubes
3 tablespoons broad beans, cooked
2 tablespoons French beans, cooked
3 tablespoons fresh peas, cooked
2 small courgettes, sliced and cooked
2 medium or 4 small carrots, sliced and cooked
1 tablespoon chopped chives
1 tablespoon chopped French parsley
4–6 tablespoons herby sour cream dressing

Above all it is crucially important not to overcook the green vegetables – 3 minutes boiling is enough. However the potatoes and the carrots do need to be cooked until they are soft enough and the hard raw edge has been taken off them. Assemble all the vegetables in the salad bowl and mix them carefully together, then add the luscious dressing.

Warm Bowls

Warm bowls are very good fun, because of the element of surprise. Your family or guests see a salad on the table and assume it is cold. The effect of the hot oil and vinegar is to slightly cook the salad ingredients which makes for a pleasing texture.

Warm Chicken Liver Salad

For 4
lettuce, preferably cabbage
350gm chicken livers, roughly chopped
150gm bacon, chopped
4 tomatoes, chopped
4 spring onions, chopped
4 tablespoons olive oil for cooking
1½ tablespoons red wine vinegar
black pepper to taste

Fry the bacon in a little oil, when half cooked add some more oil and the chicken livers. Place the torn lettuce leaves in a bowl with the chopped tomato and spring onion. Once the chicken livers are cooked add the wine vinegar to the pan – be careful it will spit – then pour all the contents on top of the salad, including any parts that have stuck to the pan. Season and then carefully turn the salad over with the salad servers so that the 'dressing' is well distributed. Serve and eat immediately. Crusty bread is essentail with this salad.

Warm Beef Stroganoff Salad

This is so quick and simple to prepare, it is cooked in minutes and is very sustaining. The lettuce does need to be crunchy, otherwise it can be overwhelmed by the richness of the other ingredients.

For 4
400gm sirloin or rump steak sliced into thin fingers
200gm mushrooms sliced
4 spring onions
½ teaspoon paprika
Cos or Webb's lettuce
3 tablespoons olive oil for cooking
1 tablespoon lemon juice
3 tablespoons soured cream
salt and black pepper to taste

Cook the steak and mushrooms in as much oil as is required, so that the steak still has a little redness showing in the middle of each finger – cooking it well done will make it too hard and spoil the blend of the ingredients. Place the lettuce, torn into large pieces into a salad bowl and when the steak is cooked to your liking, sprinkle with the paprika and then add the lemon juice – please be careful, it will spit and sizzle – followed by the soured cream. Gently toss to distribute the sauce and the steak and then decorate with the chopped spring onions. Serve and eat immediately with crusty bread to mop up the juices.

Meal in a Bowl Salads – Warm

Warm Bacon and Mushroom Salad

This is one of my favourite warm salads, based on Elizabeth David's Salade Arménienne; hers is in fact served cold, whereas this salad is warm.

For 4
lettuce or mixed leaves
350gm bacon, chopped
250gm mushrooms, sliced
4 tomatoes, chopped
2 cloves garlic, crushed
4–6 tablespoons olive oil for cooking
2 tablespoons wine vinegar
2 tablespoons chives, chopped finely
black pepper to taste

Start by preparing the bacon and the mushrooms and cooking them in a little oil – you will need to add more as you go along as it will be soaked up by the mushrooms. Place the lettuce and tomatoes in a salad bowl. Add the garlic to the bacon and mushrooms and cook for a moment to release the flavour. Add more oil to the pan, so that you can see it – this will form the basis of the dressing – now add the wine vinegar – it will spit so stand well back. Pour all the contents of the pan onto the lettuce and tomato, add the chives and black pepper (salt is not needed because of the salt in the bacon) and mix gently together so that the ingredients and dressing are well distributed. Serve immediately, with some crusty bread, while the warmth is still there.

Warm Scallops Salad

Scallops are a real treat and especially good in his salad where their sweetness is offset by the rocket, coriander and the leeks.

For 4
lettuce
a handful of rocket leaves
2 cloves garlic, crushed
16 scallops
20 cherry tomatoes, left whole
2 leeks, cleaned and sliced into 2cm pieces
1 tablespoon fresh coriander leaves, roughly chopped
4 tablespoons olive oil for cooking
2 tablespoons lemon juice
black pepper to taste

Start by placing the lettuce and rocket in a salad bowl. Gently fry the leeks in a little oil until nearly cooked, then add the garlic and the scallops and a little more oil and cook the scallops; they will take no time at all, so watch them. They are ready when the white part becomes a stronger white. Add a little more oil and then the lemon juice, which will spit, so take care. Pour onto the salad, decorate with the coriander, add black pepper as required. Serve and eat immediately to enjoy the warmth. Crusty granary bread is good with this dish.

Cold Paella

This sounds like contradiction in terms; we are so used to thinking of paella cooking quietly in large pans, but the combination of chicken and prawns with rice is good whether hot or cold. It has the great advantage of benefiting from being prepared in advance.

For 4
200gm cooked rice
4 tomatoes, chopped
½ red pepper, chopped
½ green pepper, chopped
4cm cucumber, chopped
150gm cooked prawns
300gm cooked chicken, chopped into chunks
4 spring onions, chopped
1 tablespoon French parsley, chopped
4 tablespoons basic French dressing

Mix the first seven ingredients together in a salad bowl and add the dressing. It is a good idea to allow this dish to stand for an hour to allow the flavours to mingle. When ready to eat decorate with the chopped parsley and spring onions. Bread is hardly necessary, but a glass of cool white wine would be good.

Cold Carbonara

This is a useful dish for using up leftover pasta, but is good enough to warrant cooking the pasta specially. Use a medium sized pasta like orecchiette or farfalle

For 4
250gm cooked pasta
200gm mushrooms, sliced thinly
1 avocado, chopped roughly
250gm cooked ham, diced
4 spring onions, chopped
200gm French beans, cooked and chopped into 2cm lengths
a few slithers of thinly sliced parmesan as decoration
4 tablespoons herby sour cream dressing

Mix the first six ingredients together in a salad bowl and then add the dressing, mixing gently together. Decorate with a few slithers of thinly sliced parmesan. This dish would benefit from being served with a small side dish of mixed leaves and green olives.

Best Rice Salad Ever

This is a very pretty salad with a lovely combination of colours. It could very easily be made in a much larger quantity for a party, or is useful for using up leftover ham, chicken or rice. The grapes add the element of surprise and the dressing a sense of luxury.

For 4
200gm cooked rice
100gm chicken, cooked and flaked
100gm ham, cooked and diced
150gm fresh peas, lightly cooked
2 handfuls baby spinach leaves
30 seedless grapes
2 tablespoons walnut pieces
150gm French beans, cooked and cut into 2cm lengths
20 cherry tomatoes, halved
4 spring onions, chopped
4–6 tablespoons herby sour cream dressing

This salad is simply made by mixing all the ingredients together gently, making sure that it is all touched by the dressing, but not dominated by it. If the spinach leaves seem a little large they could be torn into two or three.

Best Potato Salad Ever

This is a gutsy salad, full of strong flavours which all contrast, yet combine well together.

For 4

6 medium potatoes, cubed and cooked
½ small 250gm salami roll, cut into chunks
2 sticks celery, chopped
1 red pepper, chopped
8 cornichons, chopped
8 tinned anchovies, halved
2 tablespoons chives, chopped
4–6 tablespoons yogurt and mayonnaise dressing

Mix all the ingredients gently together in a salad bowl and leave to rest to allow the flavours to settle. A light red wine, a bowl of black olives and some foccacia would go well with this salad.

Salads with Rice, Pasta, Couscous or Potatoes

Couscous Salad

Couscous salad is wonderful to make; it is less usual than rice and pasta, yet is much quicker and easier to prepare, because it is not cooked, simply mixed with hot stock. It has a soothing taste and texture and thus acts as a good base for a variety of ingredients. The first three ingredients can be either grilled or roasted whichever is easier.

For 4
1 medium aubergine, cubed and grilled or roasted
1 red pepper, chopped and grilled or roasted
2 medium courgettes, cubed and grilled or roasted
200gm couscous
400ml hot stock
3 tablespoons tinned or sprouted chick peas
1½ tablespoons sultanas
2 tablespoons pesto from a jar or homemade
4 spring onions, chopped
16 cherry tomatoes, halved
20 olives
2 tablespoons extra virgin olive oil
1 tablespoon lemon juice
a handful rocket leaves for decoration

First soak the couscous with the hot stock. Then assemble the ingredients in a bowl, adding the pesto, oil and lemon juice at the same time. Once the couscous has cooled, fluff it up with a fork and add to the salad, mixing all together gently. Decorate with the rocket leaves.

Making a salad which incorporates leftover vegetables is great fun and, above all, easy. Having cooked some fine produce for a meal, nothing is more galling than to throw perfectly good food away, even if it is into the compost bin. Leftover vegetables must be used the next day, otherwise they will lose flavour and texture. Most vegetables lend themselves to being used in salads – potatoes are excellent for example. The simplest thing is to apply the 'Take 5' principles looking for combinations of texture, taste and colour. Balance the quantities depending upon how much leftovers you have. Usually leftover vegetables make a lunch or starter salad for 2 rather than 4. Quantities can be halved for 1. Gently mix the ingredients together and add the dressing.

Leftover Potatoes

For 2
potatoes, cut up into cubes
2 spring onions, finely chopped
4 artichoke hearts from a jar
4 radishes, sliced
2 tablespoons of prawns, defrosted – for decoration
2 tablespoons herby sour cream dressing

Leftover Leeks

For 2
leeks, cut into chunks
2 tomatoes chopped
10 black olives
2 hardboiled eggs, quartered – for decoration
2 spring onions, chopped
2 tablespoons sweet and sour tomato dressing

Salads with Leftovers – Vegetables

Leftover Broccoli

For 2

broccoli, broken into 2cm florets
salami, cut into pieces
1 stick celery, chopped
2 spring onions, chopped
3 cornichons or 2 gerkins, sliced
2 tablespoons basic French dressing

Leftover Cauliflower

For 2

cauliflower, separated into florets
1 tablespoon walnuts
2 spring onions, chopped
1 red pepper, chopped
½ teaspoon curry powder
2 tablespoons yogurt and mayonnaise dressing

Leftover Carrots

For 2

carrots, sliced or chunked
1 orange, peeled, quartered and sliced
1 dessertspoon capers
10 black olives
2 spring onions chopped
2 tablespoons basic French dressing

Leftover pasta, rice or couscous can be used as the base of any salad and will add texture and substance

Leftovers of meat, fish or chicken will naturally make a more substantial salad, unless it is only a couple of tablespoonfuls, in which case they can be added almost as a decoration to any salad. Otherwise with leftovers it depends whether you want them to dominate the salad, or whether they are to have equal weight with the other ingredients. In the end this will depend upon the quantity. The important thing is not to waste good food by throwing it away. Equally these salads are not about clearing out the bits and pieces left in the fridge over the previous week. It is important to have respect for good ingredients and to use them the next day or not at all!

Leftover Beef

For 2
beef, cubed
3cm cucumber, chopped
4 cornichons or 3 gerkins chopped
1 tablespoon sliced peppers from a jar
2 spring onions chopped
2 tablespoons herby sour cream dressing

Leftover Pork

For 2
pork, cubed
½ apple, diced
8 sunblush tomatoes from a jar
1 stick celery, chopped
2 teaspoons grain mustard
2 tablespoons basic French dressing

Salads with Leftovers – Meat, Fish or Chicken

Leftover Lamb

For 2
lamb, cubed
4 dried apricots, chopped
10 cherry tomatoes, halved
½ green pepper chopped
1 teaspoon mint, chopped
2 tablespoons basic French dressing

Leftover Chicken

For 2
chicken, cubed
10 seedless grapes
3cm cucumber chopped
1 stick celery, chopped
1 tablespoon walnut pieces
2 tablespoons yogurt and mayonnaise dressing

Leftover Fish

For 2
fish, flaked or chopped
3cm cucumber, chopped
80gm feta cheese, cubed
½ avocado diced
10 green olives
2 tablespoons basic French dressing

The store cupboard can add a touch of the exotic or surprise into your salads. As you will have noticed I use ingredients from the store cupboard to enhance my salads. There are a number of reasons for this: firstly it widens the range of contrasts available, secondly it means that you always have to hand that extra ingredient that will make the difference between a dull and an exciting salad, thirdly it means that if you only have a couple of fresh or leftover ingredients, you can still make a salad; fourthly using stored ingredients means less preparation, less chopping – good when you are in a hurry; and lastly that you can, when pushed make a salad with just your store cupboard ingredients as on p6.

Items that I try to keep in the cupboard most of the time are: bottled artichokes, olives, black, green and stuffed, sunblush tomatoes, small or ruby beetroot, peppers, capers, cornichons or gerkins, small peppers stuffed with cheese, cubes of feta cheese in oil, pickled quail eggs and Scandinavian pickled herring, both sweet and sour; tinned anchovies, small tins of tuna, tins of chick peas and mixed beans; sultanas, walnuts and pine nuts.

Very often, when using store cupboard items I start with a lettuce and add either fresh, leftover or store cupboard ingredients. The main idea is to keep it simple and balanced. Ingredients from the store cupboard often have quite strong flavours and therefore need to be used in moderation.

Again use a dressing that will enhance the contrast of flavours – items in jars are usually stored in oil or vinegar so this needs to be borne in mind when selecting a dressing – sometimes a little lemon juice is better than a dressing. All the salads are gently tossed together.

Using the Store Cupboard

Store Cupboard Salad 1

For 4

1 lettuce

12 small bottled stuffed peppers or 2 larger thinly sliced

20 olives

100gm parmesan cheese, cut thinly into shards

1 tablespoon drained tinned chick peas

2 tablespoons basic French dressing

1 tablespoon lemon juice

Store Cupboard Salad 2

For 4

1 lettuce

8 tinned anchovies, sliced into 2 or 3

2 tablespoons drained tinned mixed beans

8 pickled quail eggs, halved

8 artichoke pieces

2 tablespoons herby sour cream dressing

Store Cupboard Salad 3

For 4

1 lettuce

8 small pieces pickled fish from a jar

6 small bottled beetroot, halved

8 cornichons or 4 gerkins, chopped

2 tablespoons walnut pieces

3 tablespoons sweet and sour tomato dressing

Both the fridge and the freezer are store cupboards for other ingredients. The fridge is useful for storing meats such as bacon, small whole 250gm salamis and chorizo, packets of smoked ham – Bavarian, Parma or Serrano, also cheese: block parmesan, feta, small camemberts and goat's cheese, whether creamy or in a log. Some salad and vegetable ingredients are worth storing for a few days so that they are readily available: spring onions, cucumber, celery, cherry and medium tomatoes, red and green peppers, carrots and of course eggs. Lettuce and salad leaves will keep in the fridge for a few days, as will mushrooms, although the fewer the better. The freezer is useful for keeping prawns and small quantities of smoked salmon, both of which defrost quickly. Fridge ingredients can be used as salad additions or as the star of a salad. The quantity of salad dressing will vary according to the ingredients – the idea is to dress not drown.

Fridge Salad 1

For 4
1 cabbage lettuce, broken up and the larger leaves torn
120gm bacon, chopped and cooked
220gm mushrooms, sliced and fried with the bacon
handful of rocket leaves
1 stick celery, chopped
4 tablespoons basic French dressing

When the bacon and mushroom are cooked, put in a bowl to cool adding the dressing at once so that it soaks into the mushrooms in particular. Assemble the salad in a serving bowl, lettuce first, then bacon and mushrooms, topped by the celery and the rocket.

Fridge Salad 2

For 4
mixed leaves
120gm salami from a small roll, cut into small cubes
20 cherry tomatoes, halved
1 red pepper, chopped
3 tablespoons basic French dressing

Fridge Salad 3

For 4
mixed leaves
1 green pepper, chopped
3cm cucumber, chopped
1 stick celery, chopped
4 spring onions, chopped
3 tablespoons sweet and sour tomato dressing

Fridge Salad 4

For 4
2 Little Gem lettuces, cut in halves
1 green pepper, chopped
3cm cucumber, chopped
4 tablespoons prawns, defrosted
4 spring onions, chopped
3 tablespoons herby sour cream dressing

It is probably better if this salad is served on individual plates.

Cheese always adds an extra dimension to a salad, both in taste and texture, also a certain dryness which contrasts with the juiciness of other salad ingredients. Because cheese has a strong taste it is important not to allow it to dominate unless you intend it to; Cheese Salad 1 does this to good effect. Cheese can also be used as the surprise ingredient such as the parmesan in Store Cupboard Salad 1 (p36). I try to use local cheese whenever possible.

Eggs are a versatile ingredient, either dominant or as an accessory. Old-fashioned hardboiled eggs sliced with tomatoes are still a lovely dish and soft boiled eggs cut in half served on mixed leaves with anchovies are luscious. These are individual salads, layered with the dressing on top.

Cheese Salad 1

For 4
4 small or 2 large slices of bread, toasted with the crusts cut off
4 small Cornish camemberts or goat's cheeses
mixed leaves
16 cherry tomatoes, halved
2 tablespoons pine nuts
drizzle of olive oil
tiny drizzle thick balsamic vinegar

This salad should be served on individual plates. Take the toasted bread and place the individual cheese on top and grill for 5 minutes or bake in a hot oven for 7–8 minutes. Place the mixed leaves in individual bowls with the cherry tomatoes on top, then the cooked cheese on toast, then decorate with the pine nuts and drizzle olive oil around on the leaves and then a little balsamic vinegar just on the cheese itself for a contrast in taste and colour.

Using Cheese and Eggs

Cheese Salad 2

For 4

150gm local crumbly cheese, cubed
8 small beetroot from a jar, halved
mixed leaves
8 radishes, sliced
8 anchovies, halved
3 tablespoons yogurt and mayonnaise dressing

Layer the ingredients on top of the mixed leaves and gently spoon the dressing on top.

Egg Salad 1

For 4

4 eggs, soft boiled so the yolk is only just set, cut in half
8 anchovies cut in half
mixed leaves
16 black olives
2 red peppers chopped
3 tablespoons yogurt and mayonnaise dressing

Layer as above.

Egg Salad 2

For 4

4 eggs, hardboiled and chopped
250gm French beans, roughly chopped and cooked
mixed leaves
2 tablespoons sliced red peppers from a jar
1 medium leek – uncooked, very finely sliced
3 tablespoons basic French dressing

Layer the ingredients, finishing with the chopped egg.

The fruit bowl is another useful source of ingredients. Fruit adds a wonderful element of surprise as well as colour and texture. Just add what you have to hand: melon cubes, red currants, a few slices of fresh peach or nectarine, grapes and oranges, strawberries – sliced strawberries and cucumber with a French dressing make a pretty summer salad.

Fruit Bowl Salad 1
For 4
150gm feta cheese cubed
20 seedless grapes, halved
mixed leaves
3 tablespoons walnut pieces
1 apple, sliced thinly
1 tablespoon lemon juice
3 tablespoons basic French dressing

Layer the ingredients in one bowl on top of the mixed leaves and gently spoon the dressing on top.

Fruit Bowl Salad 2
For 4
mixed leaves or lettuce
2 oranges, peeled and sliced thinly
20 black olives
8 cornichons halved or 4 gerkins sliced
2 large slices bread, cut into cubes and fried quickly in olive oil to make croutons
¼ teaspoon hot paprika for dusting the cooked croutons
3 tablespoons basic French dressing

Layer the ingredients in one bowl on top of the mixed leaves and gently spoon the dressing on top, then add the croutons.

Sprouting Beans and Seeds

Recent additions to the salad repertoire are sprouted seeds and beans – you can buy them ready-sprouted in some supermarkets or better still sprout them yourself. They are highly nutritious and make interesting eating. My favourite sprouted beans are chick peas, aduki beans, mung beans and lentils; the sprouted seeds I prefer are white radish, black mustard seed, red clover and broccoli.

Sprouting Bean Salad

For 4
1 avocado, peeled, stoned and roughly chopped
2 tablespoons sprouted chick peas
2 tablespoons sprouted mung and/or aduki beans
4 tomatoes, chopped
1 red pepper, chopped
3 tablespoons herby sour cream dressing

Gently mix the ingredients together in a salad bowl and then add the dressing.

Sprouting Seed Salad

For 4
mixed leaves
3cm cucumber, sliced
1 carrot, grated
3 tablespoons melon, cubed
2 tablespoons red clover seeds, sprouted
2 tablespoons white radish seeds, sprouted
3 tablespoons basic French dressing

Mix the first 4 ingredients together in a salad bowl, add the dressing and then decorate with the sprouted seeds.

Celebratory salads are about delighting in the abundance of salad vegetables as the seasons pass. We are lucky in the Southwest to have a rich variety of vegetables available locally through the year; it is very important to me to use them as they come into season, even if it means eating them frequently and then not to regret their passing.

Celebratory Asparagus Salad

Asparagus is only available for about 6 weeks, so it is important to use it as much as possible. The larger spears can be the focus of a salad, while the thinner spears can be used as an ingredient in a meal in a bowl salad or a pasta or rice salad.

For 4
24 large asparagus spears
a few mixed leaves
1 tablespoon chives, chopped
4 thin slices smoked salmon, roughly sliced
1 tablespoon lemon juice.
4 tablespoons basic French dressing

This salad can be served on individual plates or one large platter. Use the mixed leaves as a base. Carefully cook the asparagus so that it is just cooked, drain, refresh under a cold tap, so that it is warm, rather than hot. Place the asparagus on top of the leaves, decorate with the smoked salmon and chives; spoon the lemon juice over the smoked salmon to take away the oiliness of the fish and then spoon the French dressing over all.

Celebratory Tomato Salad

Tomatoes are common in salads, but when you have some just fresh from the plant their lusciousness needs celebrating.

For 4
12 very fresh tomatoes, finely sliced
a few sprigs of basil leaves, torn
2 tablespoons chives, finely chopped
½ tablespoon mint, finely chopped
4 tablespoons basic French dressing

Carefully place the tomatoes on top of the mixed leaves on a large dish. Decorate with the herbs and spoon the dressing over. It is essential to leave the dish for an hour so that the flavours mingle before you serve with crusty bread to soak up the juices.

Celebratory Vegetable Salad

This warm bowl salad celebrates vegetables. Here the delicate flavours contrast and blend, without the dominance of meat.

For 4
16 small new potatoes or 8 larger halved
300gm broad beans and peas, podded
200gm sugar snap peas and runner beans, sliced
4 small courgettes, cut into chunks
8 thin asparagus spears, cut in half
4 tomatoes, roughly chopped
mixed chives, mint and parsley, chopped
4–6 tablespoons basic French dressing

Cook the potatoes in a large saucepan; when nearly ready add the green vegetables for 3 minutes. Drain and place in a serving bowl, add the tomatoes, herbs and dressing. Enjoy!